PIMLICO

801

ON TRUTH

Harry G. Frankfurt is professor emeritus of philosophy at Princeton University. His books include *On Bullshit*; *The Reasons of Love*; *Necessity, Volition, and Love*; *The Importance of What We Care About*; and *Demons, Dreamers, and Madmen*. He lives in Princeton, New Jersey.

ON TRUTH

HARRY G. FRANKFURT

PIMLICO

Published by Pimlico 2007

2 4 6 8 10 9 7 5 3 1

Copyright © Harry G. Frankfurt 2006

Harry G. Frankfurt has asserted his right under the Copyright,
Designs and Patents Act 1988 to be identified as the author of this work

First published in the United States by Alfred A. Knopf,
a division of Random House, Inc.,
New York, and in Canada by Random House of Canada Limited, Toronto

First published in Great Britain in 2007 by
Pimlico

Pimlico
Random House, 20 Vauxhall Bridge Road,
London SW1V 2SA

www.randomhouse.co.uk

Addresses for companies within The Random House Group Limited can be
found at: www.randomhouse.co.uk

The Random House Group Limited Reg. No. 954009

A CIP catalogue record for this book
is available from the British Library

ISBN 9781845951245

The Random House Group Limited makes every effort to ensure that the papers
used in its books are made from trees that have been legally sourced from well-
managed and credibly certified forests. Our paper procurement policy can be
found at: www.randomhouse.co.uk/paper.htm

Printed and bound in Germany by GGP Media GmbH, Pößneck

For Joan, again
It was, after all, her idea

ON TRUTH

INTRODUCTION

Not very long ago, I published an essay on bullshit, entitled *On Bullshit* (Princeton University Press, 2005). In that essay, I offered a provisional analysis of the concept of bullshit: that is, I specified the conditions that I considered to be both necessary and sufficient for applying the concept correctly. My claim was that bullshitters, although they represent themselves as being engaged simply in conveying information, are not engaged in that enterprise at all. Instead, and most essentially, they are fakers and phonies who are attempting by what they say to manipulate the opinions and the attitudes of those to whom they speak. What they care about primarily, therefore, is whether what they say is *effective* in accomplishing this manipulation. Correspondingly, they are more or less indifferent to whether what they say is true or whether it is false.

In that book, I also addressed a number of other issues. I explored the distinction, which is fundamentally important though generally left unexamined, between bullshit and lies. I made a few tentative suggestions concerning how to account for the extraordinary prevalence and persistence of bullshit in our culture. And I argued that bullshitting constitutes a more insidious threat than lying does to the conduct of civilized life.

At the time, that seemed like enough. I realized later, however, that I had paid no attention at all in my book to an issue with which any adequate discussion of bullshit must certainly deal. I had made an important assumption, which I had offhandedly supposed most of my readers would share: viz., being indifferent to truth is an undesirable or even a reprehensible characteristic, and bullshitting is therefore to be avoided and condemned. But I had entirely omitted to provide anything like a careful and convincing explanation—indeed, I had omitted any explanation at all—of exactly why truth actually *is* so important to us, or why we should especially care about it.

In other words, I had failed to explain why indifference to truth, which I had claimed to be distinctive of bullshit, is such a bad thing. Of course, most people do recognize, and will more or less readily acknowledge, that truth has considerable importance. On the other hand, few people are prepared to offer much real illumination of just what it is that makes truth so important.

We are all aware that our society perennially sustains enormous infusions—some deliberate, some merely incidental—of bullshit, lies, and other forms of misrepresentation and deceit. It is apparent, however, that this burden has somehow failed—at least, so far—to cripple our civilization. Some people may perhaps take this complacently to show that truth is not so important after all, and that there is no particularly strong reason for us to care much about it. In my opinion, that would be a deplorable mistake. Accordingly, I propose to consider here—as a sort of sequel to *On Bullshit,* or as an inquiry to which that work might serve as prolegomenon—the practical and theoretical importance that truth actually enjoys, whether or not we generally act as though we recognize that it does so.

My editor (the inimitable and indispensable George Andreou) has pointed out to me the rather paradoxical circumstance that, while no one has any trouble recognizing that there is plenty of *bullshit* around, quite a few people remain stubbornly unwilling to acknowledge that there might be—even in principle—such a thing as *truth*. In my discussion, however, I shall not even try—at least not by any directly confrontational argument or analysis—to settle once and for all the entangled debate between those who accept the reality of a meaningful distinction between being true and being false and those who energetically represent themselves (never mind whether they are correct in doing so, or whether it is even *possible* that they should be correct) as denying that the distinction is a valid one or that it corresponds to any objective reality. That debate seems unlikely ever to be finally resolved, and it is generally unrewarding.

In any case, even those who profess to deny the validity or the objective reality of the true-false

distinction continue to maintain
without apparent embarrassment that
this denial is a position that they do
truly endorse. The statement that they
reject the distinction between true
and false is, they insist, an unquali-
fiedly *true* statement about their
beliefs, *not* a *false* one. This prima
facie incoherence in the articulation
of their doctrine makes it uncertain
precisely how to construe what it is
that they propose to deny. It is also
enough to make us wonder just how
seriously we need to take their claim
that there is no objectively meaningful or worthwhile distinction to be
made between what is true and what
is false.

I am also going to avoid the for-
bidding complexities that overhang
any conscientious effort to *define* the

notions of truth and falsity. This would likely be another discouraging and unnecessarily distracting task. So I will simply take for granted the more or less universally accepted commonsense ways of understanding these notions. We all know what it means to tell the truth about various things with which we are authoritatively familiar—for example, such things as our names and addresses. We understand with equal clarity, moreover, what it means to give false accounts of such things. We know quite well how to lie about them.

Accordingly, I shall assume that my readers are comfortably at home with these unpretentious and philosophically innocent commonsense understandings of the difference between being true and being false.

They may not be able to define the
notions with unassailable accuracy
and formal precision. I shall take it
for granted, however, that they are
able to carry on more or less intelligently and confidently with them.

One more thing. My discussion
will be concerned exclusively with
the value and the importance of *truth,*
and not at all with the value or the
importance of our *efforts to find* truth
or of our *experience in finding* it. Coming to recognize that the evidence for
a certain proposition is conclusive,
and that there can be no further
reasonable question of whether the
proposition is true, frequently brings
with it a gratified feeling of decisive
completion and success, and sometimes the recognition may even be
rather thrilling. A rigorous demon-

stration unequivocally resolves all reasonable uncertainty concerning the proposition's truth; hence, naturally, all resistance to accepting the proposition evaporates. This is liberating and refreshing. It frees us from the anxieties and inhibitions of doubt, and it enables us to stop worrying about what to believe. Our minds become more settled, finally relaxed and confident.

Experiences of this sort are more or less familiar to scholars and scientists. They are also known to numerous laymen, who may often enough encounter them in the ordinary conduct of their business. Many people are introduced to them in their high school geometry classes, when they are led to appreciate the impeccable demonstration of some Euclidean theorem, and thus to *see* clearly and distinctly that the theorem has been *conclusively proved.*

Despite the relatively widespread enjoyment of these experiences, and regardless of their unmistakable interest and value, I shall not discuss them any further. As I said earlier, my attention will be focused uniquely on the value and the importance to us of truth. I shall not be concerned with the value or the importance of our experience in establishing, or in trying to discover, what is true. My topic is not the process of inquiry, or the occasion of its successful completion, but its target.

With these preliminary stipulations and reservations in place, let us begin. Is truth something that in fact we do—and should—especially care about? Or is the love of truth, as professed by so many distinguished thinkers and writers, itself merely another example of bullshit?

I

When I try to put my finger on just why truth is important to us, what comes most readily to my mind is a thought that may perhaps seem unpromisingly banal but that is, nevertheless, unquestionably pertinent. It is the thought that truth often possesses very considerable practical utility. Any society that manages to be even minimally functional must have, it seems to me, a robust appreciation of the endlessly protean utility of truth. After all, how could a society that cared too little for truth make sufficiently well-informed judgments and decisions concerning the most suitable disposition of its public business? How could it possibly flourish, or even survive, without knowing enough about relevant facts to pursue its ambitions successfully and to cope prudently and effectively with its problems?

It seems even more clear to me that higher levels of civilization must depend even more heavily on a conscientious respect for the importance of honesty and clarity in reporting the facts, and on a stubborn concern for accuracy in determining what the facts are. The natural and the social sciences, as well as the conduct of public affairs, surely cannot prosper except insofar as they carefully maintain this respect and this concern. The same holds for both the practical and the fine arts.

We live at a time when, strange to say, many quite cultivated individuals consider truth to be unworthy of any particular respect. It is well known, of course, that a cavalier attitude toward truth is more or less endemic within the ranks of publicists and politicians, breeds whose exemplars characteristically luxuriate in the production of bullshit, of lies, and of whatever other modes of fraudulence and fakery they are able to devise. That is old news, and we are accustomed to it.

Recently, though, a similar version of this attitude—or, indeed, a more extreme version of it—has become

disturbingly widespread even within
what might naively have been thought
to be a more reliable class of people.
Numerous unabashed skeptics and
cynics about the importance of truth
(or about the related importance of
long-established strictures against
plagiarism) have been found among
best-selling and prize-winning
authors, among writers for leading
newspapers, and among hitherto
respected historians, biographers,
memoirists, theorists of literature,
novelists—and even among philosophers, who of all people might reasonably have been counted on to
know better.

  These shameless antagonists of
common sense—members of a certain emblematic subgroup of them

call themselves "postmodernists"—
rebelliously and self-righteously deny
that truth has any genuinely objective
reality at all. They therefore go on
to deny that truth is worthy of any
obligatory deference or respect.
Indeed, they emphatically dismiss a
presumption that is not only utterly
fundamental to responsible inquiry
and thought, but that would seem
to be—on the face of it—entirely
innocuous: the presumption that
"what the facts are" is a useful notion,
or that it is, at the very least, a notion
with intelligible meaning. As for the
entitlements to deference and to
respect that we ordinarily assign to
fact and to truth, the postmodernists'
view is that in the end the assignment
of those entitlements is just up for

grabs. It is simply a matter, they insist, of how you look at things.

Needless to say, all of us do quite often, conscientiously and confidently, identify certain propositions as true and others as false. Postmodernist thinkers are undaunted, however, by the undeniably ubiquitous acceptance of this practice. Somewhat more surprisingly, they are not disconcerted even by its often valuable outcomes and consequences. The reason for this impermeable obduracy is that, according to the postmodernists' line of thought, the distinctions that we make between what is true and what is false are ultimately guided by nothing more indisputably objective, or more compellingly authoritative, than our individual points of view. Or, on another variant of the doctrine, it is not so much personal perspectives that call the shots; more particularly, the shots are called by constraints that are *imposed* on all of us, either by stringent economic and political requirements or by the powerfully motivating habits and customs of our society. The point on which the post-modernists especially rely is just this: what a person *regards* as true either is a function merely of the person's individual point of view or is determined by what the person is *constrained to regard* as true by various complex and inescapable social pressures.

This point strikes me as being not only far too glib but also rather obtuse. Surely it is unquestionable, regardless of what postmodernists or anyone else may say, that engineers and architects, for instance, must strive to achieve—and do at times succeed in achieving—genuine objectivity. Many of them are extremely skilled at assessing, with generally reliable accuracy, both the obstacles that are inherent to the implementation of their plans and the resources that are available to them for coping with those obstacles. The carefully executed measurements that are vital to their designs and constructions cannot at all plausibly be thought of as being subject to the shifting variations and the mindless vagaries that a dependency upon individual perspective would imply; nor would it be any more plausible to think of them as being subject to the frequently arbitrary or irrelevant demands of social discipline and taboo. They must obviously be precise, but precision is not enough. The measurements must be stable, under whatever conditions and from whatever point of view they are made, and they must be correct.

Suppose that a bridge collapses under no more than normal stress. What would that tell us? It would tell us, at a minimum, that those who designed or who constructed the bridge made some pretty bad mistakes. It would be obvious to us that at least some of the solutions that they had devised, in dealing with the multiple problems they confronted, were fatally incorrect.

The same applies, of course, in medicine. Physicians must endeavor to make sound judgments concerning how to deal with illness and injury. Accordingly, they need to know which medicines and which procedures can confidently be expected to help their patients; they need to know which are in fact unlikely to do any real good, and they need to know which are likely to be harmful.

No one in his right mind would rely on a builder, or submit to the care of a physician, who does not care about the truth. Even writers, artists, and musicians must—in their own ways—know how to get things right. They must at least be able to avoid getting them too far wrong. In the course of their creative work, they invariably encounter significant problems—for instance, problems of

technique and of style. Certain ways
of dealing with these problems are
clearly far superior to others. Perhaps
no way of dealing with any of them is
indisputably and uniquely correct.
However, many of the alternatives are
manifestly *in*correct. Indeed, some
are recognizable, immediately and
uncontroversially, as truly awful.

In all of these contexts, there is a
clear difference between getting
things right and getting them wrong,
and thus a clear difference between
the true and the false. It is frequently
claimed, to be sure, that the situation
is different when it comes to histori-
cal analyses and to social commen-
taries, and especially when it comes
to the evaluations of people and of
policies that these analyses and com-

mentaries generally include. The argument ordinarily offered in support of this claim is that such evaluations are always heavily influenced by the personal circumstances and attitudes of the people who make them, and that for this reason we cannot expect works of history or of social commentary to be rigorously impartial and objective.

Admittedly, the element of subjectivity in such matters is inescapable. There are important limits, however, to what this admission implies concerning the range of variation in interpreting the facts that serious historians, for instance, may be expected to display. There is a dimension of reality into which even the boldest—or the laziest—indulgence of subjectivity cannot dare to intrude.

This is the spirit of Georges Clemenceau's famous response, when he was asked to speculate as to what future historians would say about the First World War: "They will not say that Belgium invaded Germany."

II

Still, many people manage to convince themselves—sometimes rather smugly—that normative (i.e., evaluative) judgments cannot properly be regarded as being *either* true *or* false. Their view is that a judgment of that kind does not actually make any factual claim at all—i.e., any claim that *would* be either correct or incorrect. Rather, they believe, such judgments only express personal feelings and attitudes that are, strictly speaking, *neither* true *nor* false.

Okay. Suppose we concede this. It remains clear nonetheless that accepting or rejecting an evaluative judgment must depend on other judgments that are themselves straightforwardly nonnormative— i.e., on statements about facts. Thus, we cannot reasonably judge for ourselves that a certain person has a bad moral character except on the basis of factual statements describing instances of his or her behavior that seem to provide concrete evidence of moral deficiency. Moreover, these factual statements concerning the person's behavior must be true, and the reasoning by which we derive our evaluative judgment from them must be valid. Otherwise, neither the statements nor the reasoning can effectively help to justify the conclusion. They will do nothing to show that the evaluation resting on them is reasonable.

So the distinction between what is true and what is false remains critically pertinent to our assessments of evaluative or normative judgments, even if it is agreed that the true-false distinction has no direct application to those judgments themselves. We may admit, if we consider it wise to do so, that the evaluations we make are neither true nor false. However, we cannot admit a similar characterization of the factual statements, or of the reasoning, with which we must attempt to support those evaluations.

In the same way, statements of fact are indispensable in explaining and in

validating the purposes and goals that
we choose and that we set ourselves
to pursue. Of course, many thinkers
deny that our selection of purposes
and goals—at least, of those that are
not selected merely for their instrumental value in helping us to achieve
more ultimate ambitions—can be
justified rationally at all. Rather, they
insist, we adopt purposes and goals
solely by virtue of what we happen to
feel or to desire.

Surely it is apparent, however,
that in large part we select the objects
that we desire, that we love, and to
which we commit ourselves, because
of what we *believe* about them—for
instance, that they will increase our
wealth or protect our health, or
that they will serve our interests in

some other way. Hence, the truth or the falsity of the factual statements on which we rely in explaining or in validating our choice of goals and our commitments is inescapably relevant to the rationality of our attitudes and our choices. Unless we know whether we are justified in regarding various factual judgments as true, we cannot know whether there is really any sense in feeling and in choosing as we do.

For these reasons, no society can afford to despise or to disrespect the truth. It is not enough, however, for a society merely to acknowledge that truth and falsity are, when all is said and done, legitimate and significant concepts. In addition, the society must not neglect to provide encouragement and support for capable individuals who devote themselves to acquiring and to exploiting significant truths. Moreover, whatever benefits and rewards it may sometimes be possible to attain by bullshitting, by dissembling, or through sheer mendacity, societies cannot afford to tolerate anyone or anything that fosters a slovenly indifference to the distinction between true and false. Much less can they indulge the shabby, narcissistic pretense that being true to the facts is less important than being "true to oneself." If there is any attitude that is *inherently* antithetical to a decent and orderly social life, that is it.

A society that is recklessly and persistently remiss in any of these

ways is bound to decline or, at least,
to render itself culturally inert. It will
certainly be incapable of any substan-
tial achievement, and even of any
coherent and prudent ambition.
Civilizations have *never* gotten along
healthily, and *cannot* get along healthily, without large quantities of *reliable
factual information*. They also cannot
flourish if they are beset with trouble-
some infections of *mistaken* beliefs. To
establish and to sustain an advanced
culture, we need to avoid being
debilitated either by error or by
ignorance. We need to know—and,
of course, we must also understand
how to make productive use of—
a great many truths.

   This is not only a societal imperative. It also applies to each of us, as
individuals. Individuals require truths

in order to negotiate their way effectively through the thicket of hazards
and opportunities that all people
invariably confront in going about
their lives. They need to know the
truth about what to eat and what not
to eat, about how to dress (given the
facts concerning climatic conditions),
about where to live (in view of information about such things as tectonic
fault lines, the prevalence of ava-
lanches, and the proximity of shops,
jobs, and schools), as well as about
how to do what they are paid to do,
how to raise their children, what to
think of the people they meet, what
they are capable of achieving, what
they would like to achieve, and an
endless variety of other mundane
yet vital matters.

    Our success or failure in whatever

we undertake, and therefore in life altogether, depends on whether we are guided by truth or whether we proceed in ignorance or on the basis of falsehood. It also depends critically, of course, on *what we do with* the truth. *Without* truth, however, we are out of luck before we even start.

We really cannot live without truth. We need truth not only in order to understand how to live well, but in order to know how to survive at all. Furthermore, this is something that we cannot easily fail to notice. We are therefore bound to recognize, at least implicitly, that truth is important to us; and, consequently, we are also bound to understand (again, at least implicitly) that truth is not a feature of belief to which we can permit ourselves to be indifferent. Indifference would be a matter not just of negligent imprudence. It would quickly prove fatal. To the extent that we appreciate its importance to us, then, we cannot reasonably allow ourselves to refrain either from wanting the truth about many things or from striving to possess it.

III

But, one might well ask: since when has *being reasonable* meant very much to us? It is notorious that we humans have a talent, which we frequently display, for ignoring and evading the requirements of rationality. How, then, can it be considered at all likely that we will respect and accede to the rational imperative that we take truth seriously?

Before we give up on ourselves too hastily, let me introduce into the discussion some pertinent (and, I hope, helpful) thoughts of a remarkable seventeenth-century Portuguese-Dutch-Jewish philosopher: Baruch Spinoza. Spinoza maintained that regardless of whether we enjoy, feel comfortable with, or cherish the species of rationality that is at issue here, that kind of rationality will be *imposed* on us. Whether we like it or not, we really *cannot help* submitting to it. We are *driven* to do so, as Spinoza understood the matter, by *love.*

Spinoza explained the nature of love as follows: "Love is nothing but Joy with the accompanying idea of an external cause" (*Ethics,* part III, proposition 13, scholium). As for the meaning of "joy," he stipulated that it is "what follows that passion by which the . . . [individual] passes to a greater perfection" (*Ethics,* part III, proposition 11, scholium).

I suppose that many readers will find these rather opaque dicta quite uninviting. They do truly seem forbiddingly obscure. Even apart from this barrier to making productive use of Spinoza's thoughts, moreover, one might not unreasonably question whether he was qualified, in the first place, to speak with any particular authority about love. After all, he had no children, he never married, and it seems that he never even had a steady girlfriend.

Of course, these details concerning his personal life have no plausible relevance except to questions about his authority with respect to romantic, to marital, and to parental love.

What Spinoza was actually thinking of
when he wrote about love, however,
was none of these. In fact, he was not
thinking especially of any variety of
love that necessarily has *a person* as its
object. Let me try to explain what I
believe he did have in mind.

Spinoza was convinced that every
individual has an essential nature that
it strives, throughout its existence, to
realize and to sustain. In other words,
he believed that there is in each individual an underlying innate impetus
to become, and to remain, what that
individual most essentially is. When
Spinoza wrote of "that passion by
which the . . . [individual] passes to
a greater perfection," he was referring to an externally caused (hence a
"passion"—i.e., a change in the indi-

vidual that does not come about by
his own action, but rather a change
with respect to which he is *passive*)
augmentation of the individual's
capacities for surviving and for devel-
oping in fulfillment of his essential
nature. Whenever the capacities of
an individual for attaining these goals
are increased, the increase in the
individual's power to attain them is
accompanied by a sense of enhanced
vitality. The individual is aware of a
more vigorously expansive ability
to become and to continue as what
he most truly is. Thus, he feels more
fully himself. He feels more fully
alive.

Spinoza supposes (plausibly
enough, I think) that this experience
of an increase in vitality—this aware-

ness of an expanding ability to realize
and to sustain one's true nature—is
inherently exhilarating. The exhilaration may perhaps be comparable to
the exhilaration that a person often
experiences as an accompaniment
to invigorating physical exercise,
in which the person's lungs, heart,
and muscular capacities are exerted
more strenuously than usual. When
working out energetically, people
frequently feel more completely and
more vividly alive than they do before exercising, when they are less
fully and less directly aware of their
own capacities, when they are less
brimming with a sense of their own
vitality. I believe it is an experience
something like this that Spinoza has in
mind when he speaks of "joy"; joy, as

I think he understands it, is a feeling
of the enlargement of one's power to
live, and to continue living, in accord
with one's most authentic nature.

Now, if a person who experiences
joy recognizes that the joy has a certain external cause—that is, if the
person identifies someone or something as the object to which he *owes*
his joy and on which his joy *depends*—
Spinoza believes that the person inevitably *loves* that object. This is what
he understands love to be: the way
we respond to what we recognize as
causing us joy. On his account, then,
people cannot help loving whatever
they recognize as being, for them,
a source of joy. They invariably love
what they believe helps them to continue in existence and to become
more fully themselves. It seems to

me that Spinoza is at least on the right track here. Many paradigmatic instances of love do exhibit, more or less straightforwardly, the pattern that he defines: people do tend to love what they feel helps them to "find themselves," to discover "who they really are," and to face life successfully without betraying or compromising their fundamental natures.

To his account of the essential nature of love, Spinoza adds an observation about love that also seems accurate: "One who loves necessarily strives to have present and preserve the things he loves" (*Ethics,* part III, proposition 11, scholium). The things that a person loves are manifestly and necessarily precious to him. His life, and both his attainment and his continued enjoyment of personal authenticity, depend on them. Therefore, he naturally takes care to protect them and to ensure that they are readily available to him.

Spinoza believed it follows from this that people cannot help loving truth. They cannot help doing so, he thought, because they cannot help recognizing that truth is indispensable in enabling them to stay alive, to understand themselves, and to live fully in accord with their own natures. Without access to truths concerning their own individual natures, their particular capacities and needs, and the availability and correct use of the resources that they require in order to survive and to flourish, people would have very serious difficulty with their lives.

They would be unable even to design
appropriate goals for themselves,
much less to pursue those goals effectively. They would be pretty much
helpless, in fact, to keep themselves
going at all.

Therefore, Spinoza maintained, a
person who despises or who is indifferent to truth must be a person who
despises or who is indifferent to his
own life. Such a hostile or careless
attitude toward oneself is extremely
rare, and it is difficult to sustain.
Thus, Spinoza concluded that nearly
everyone—everyone who values and
who cares about his own life—does,
whether knowingly or not, love
truth. So far as I can see, Spinoza
was on the whole correct about this.
Practically all of us do love truth,

whether or not we are aware that we do so. And, to the extent that we recognize what dealing effectively with the problems of life entails, we cannot help loving truth.

IV

What I have been dealing with so far, in my discussion of truth, is essentially a pragmatic—i.e., a consequential or utilitarian—consideration. It is a consideration, moreover, that has to do with "truth" as understood *distributively*—i.e., not as referring to an entity of some mysterious sort that might be identified and examined as a separate reality in its own right, but rather as a characteristic that belongs to (or that is "distributed" among) any number of individual propositions and that can be encountered only as it characterizes one or another true proposition. The consideration with which I have been dealing pertains to the *usefulness* of many truths in facilitating the successful design and pursuit of social or individual ambitions and activities, a usefulness that those truths possess only by virtue of *being* true. This utility is a feature of truths that is easy to grasp, difficult to overlook, and quite impossible for any sensible person to deny. It provides the most obvious and the most elementary reason for people to care about truth—about the characteristic of being true—and to regard it as being important to them.

Let us make an effort now to go a little farther. We may be able to expand our appreciation of the importance of truth by considering a

question that arises quite naturally,
in one form or another, when we
begin to reflect on the obvious pragmatic utility of truth. How is it that
truths possess this utility? What is
the explanatory connection between
the fact that they are true and the
fact that they have so much practical
value? For that matter, why are truths
useful at all?

The question is not very difficult to
answer. At least, it is easy enough to
see how to *begin* answering it. When
we are engaged in active life, or when
we attempt to plan and to manage
our various practical affairs, we are
undertaking to cope with *reality*
(some of this reality being of our own
making, most of it not). The outcomes of our efforts—as well as the

value to us of those outcomes—will depend, at least in part, on the properties of the real objects and events with which we are dealing. They will depend on what those real objects and events are like, on how they fit into our interests, and on how, given their causally relevant features, they respond to what we do.

Insofar as truths possess instrumental value, they do so because they capture and convey the nature of these realities. Truths have practical utility because they consist of, and because they therefore can provide us with, accurate accounts of the properties (including, especially, the causal powers and potentialities) of the real objects and events with which we must deal when we act.

We can act confidently, with a

reasonable expectation of success, only if we have enough relevant information. We need to know enough about what we are doing, and about the problems and opportunities that are likely to turn up along our way. Knowing enough is a matter here of knowing enough about the facts—that is, about the realities—that are critically pertinent to our current projects and concerns. It is, in other words, a matter of knowing as much of the truth about those realities as is necessary in order for us intelligently to formulate and to accomplish our goals.

When we have grasped these truths—that is, when we have recognized that they *are* true—we have thereby apprehended what those aspects of the world that are currently of particular interest to us are really like. This enables us to appreciate what possibilities are truly available to us, what dangers and risks we are up against, and what it is reasonable for us to expect. In other words, it makes it possible for us—at least, up to a point—to know our way around.

Now, the relevant facts are what they are regardless of what we may happen to believe about them, and regardless of what we may wish them to be. This is, indeed, the essence and the defining character of factuality, of being real: the properties of reality, and accordingly the truths about its properties, are what they are, inde-pendent of any direct or immediate control by our will. We cannot alter the facts nor, similarly, can we affect

the truth about the facts, merely by
an exercise of judgment or by an
impulse of desire.

Insofar as we know the truth, we
are in a position to be guided authoritatively in our conduct by the character of reality itself. The facts—the
true nature of reality—are the final
and incontrovertible recourse of
inquiry. They dictate and support an
ultimately decisive resolution and
rebuttal of all uncertainties and
doubts. When I was a child, I often
felt oppressed by the chaotic jumble
of implausible notions and beliefs that
I felt various adults were attempting
to foist on me. My own dedication to
truth originated, so far as I am able
to recall, in the liberating conviction
that once I grasped the truth, I would

no longer be distracted or disturbed by anyone's (including my own) speculations, hunches, or hopes.

To the extent that we grasp the truths that we need to know, we can develop sensible judgments concerning what we would like to happen, and concerning the outcomes to which various possible courses of action will probably lead. This is because we are then more or less fully aware of what we are dealing with, and because we know how the objects and events that would be implicated in our following one course of action or another will respond to what we do. In a certain part of the world, we are therefore able to move about feeling somewhat more relaxed and secure. We know what the important constituents of our environment are, we know where to find them, and we can maneuver freely without bumping into things. In that region of the world, we can begin—so to speak—to feel ourselves at home.

Needless to say, the "home" in which we find ourselves may not be a very attractive or inviting locale. It may be riddled with terrifying pitfalls and traps. The realities that it will require us to confront may be both dangerous and ugly. Far from our being fully confident in facing what awaits us, we may have no confidence whatever that we will succeed in negotiating it effectively, or even that we will be able to get through it alive.

Some people would advise us that there may be realities so frightening, or so discouraging and demoralizing, that we would be better off not knowing anything about them. In my judgment, however, it is nearly always more advantageous to *face* the facts with which we must deal than to remain ignorant of them. After all, hiding our eyes from reality will not cause any reduction of its dangers and threats; plus, our chances of dealing successfully with the hazards that it presents will surely be greater if we can bring ourselves to see things straight.

This applies no less to the truth about our own inner tendencies and character, I believe, than to the realities of the world external to us. We need to recognize what it is that we really want, what will most fully satisfy us, and what anxieties most intractably block us from acting as we would like. Genuine self-knowledge is, no doubt, exceptionally difficult to attain, and the truth about what we are may certainly be distressing. In our efforts to conduct our lives successfully, however, a readiness to face disturbing facts about ourselves may be an even more critical asset than a competent understanding merely of what we are up against in the outside world.

Without truth, either we have no opinion at all concerning how things are or our opinion is wrong. One way or the other, we do not know what kind of situation we are in. We don't know what's going on, either in the world around us or within ourselves. If we do have some relevant beliefs about these matters, they are mistaken; and false beliefs, naturally, do not effectively help us to cope. Perhaps we may be, for a time, *blissfully* ignorant or *happily* deceived, and in those ways, despite all of the difficulties that endanger us, we may temporarily avoid being especially upset or disturbed. In the end, however, our ignorance and our false beliefs are likely just to make our circumstances worse.

The problem with ignorance and error is, of course, that they leave us in the dark. Lacking the truths that we require, we have nothing to guide us but our own feckless speculations or fantasies and the importunate and unreliable advice of others. As we plan our conduct, we can therefore do no better than to spin out uninformed guesses and, shakily, to hope for the best. We do not know where we are. We are flying blind. We can proceed only very tentatively, feeling our way.

This mindless groping may work well enough for a while. Inevitably, however, it will lead us finally to blunder into trouble. We do not know enough to avoid, or to overcome, the obstacles and the dangers that we are bound to encounter. Indeed, we are doomed to remain entirely unaware of them until it is too late. And at that point, of course, we will learn of them only by virtue of our recognition that we have already been defeated.

V

Human beings are, by ancient defini-
tion, rational animals. Rationality is
our most distinctive characteristic.
It differentiates us essentially from
creatures of all other kinds. Moreover, we have a powerful inclination,
and we have convinced ourselves that
we also have some convincing reason,
to regard our rationality as making
us superior to them. It is, in any case,
the characteristic of which we humans
are most insistently and most stubbornly proud.

However, we could not properly

consider ourselves to be functioning
rationally at all if we did not acknowledge the difference between being
true and being false. To be rational is
fundamentally a matter of being
appropriately responsive to reasons.
Now, reasons are constituted of facts:
the fact that it is raining constitutes a
reason—not necessarily, of course,
a conclusive reason—for individuals
who are in the region where it is
raining, and who prefer to remain
dry, to carry umbrellas. Any rational
person who understands both what
rain is and what umbrellas do will
recognize this. To make the same
point a bit differently: the fact that it
is raining in a certain region means
that there is a reason for people in
that region to carry umbrellas if they
wish to avoid getting wet.

Only if it is *truly* a fact that it is raining in the specified region—and so, only if the statement "it is raining in the region at issue" is *true*—can either the fact of the matter or the statement thereof give anyone a reason to carry an umbrella. False statements provide no rational support for anything; they cannot effectively serve anyone as reasons. Of course, a person might display his intellectual virtuosity by drawing out (i.e., deducing) the implications of false statements—by showing, in other words, what conclusions those statements *would* rationally warrant *if* they were actually true *rather than* false. This display of agility and power in deductive reasoning might be an entertaining and even, perhaps, an impressive exercise; it might possibly serve, as well, to nourish in its performer a certain insubstantial, hollow vanity. Under ordinary conditions, however, there would not be much point to it.

The notions of truth and of factuality are indispensable, then, for imbuing the exercise of rationality with meaningful substance. They are indispensable even for understanding the very concept of rationality itself. Without them, the concept would have no meaning, and rationality itself (whatever it might turn out to be, if anything, in such deprived conditions) would be of very little use. We cannot think of ourselves as creatures whose rationality endows us with an especially significant advantage over others—indeed, we cannot think of ourselves as rational creatures at

all—unless we think of ourselves as
creatures who recognize that facts,
and true statements about the facts,
are indispensable in providing us with
reasons for believing (or for not believing) various things and for taking
(or for not taking) various actions.
If we have no respect for the distinction between true and false, we may
as well kiss our much-vaunted
"rationality" good-bye.

VI

There is evidently a close relationship between the notion of truth and the notion of factuality. For every fact, there is a true statement that relates it; and every true statement relates a fact. There are also close relationships between the notion of *truth* and the notions of *trust* and of *confidence*. These relationships are revealed etymologically when we consider the rather conspicuous similarity between the word "truth" and the somewhat archaic English word "troth." (References to etymology often herald bullshitting; but bear with me, or, if you prefer, look it up yourself.)

Although it is no longer current usage, we do still commonly understand that in the ceremonies of betrothal and of marriage the man and the woman may undertake to "pledge their *troth*" to each other. What does it mean when each pledges his or her *troth* to the other? It means that each promises to be *true* to the other. The two individuals commit themselves mutually to fulfill various expectations and requirements that are defined by morality or by local custom. Each gives an assurance to the other that he or she can confidently be *trusted* to be *true,* at least so far as concerns the fulfillment of those particular requirements and expectations.

Of course, it is not only in the contexts of betrothal and of marriage that it is important for people to trust one another. Social and communal relationships generally, in their multifarious versions and modes, can be efficient and harmonious only if people have a reasonable degree of confidence that others are on the whole reliable. If people were generally dishonest and untrustworthy, the very possibility of peaceful and productive social life would be threatened.

This has moved some philosophers to insist, with considerable vehemence, that lying decisively undermines the cohesion of human society.

Immanuel Kant, for example,
declared that "without truth social
intercourse and conversation become
valueless" *(Lectures on Ethics)*. And he
argued that because lying does
threaten society in this way, "a lie
always harms another; if not some
particular man, still it harms mankind
generally" ("On a Supposed Right to
Lie from Altruistic Motives"). Michel
Montaigne made a similar claim:
"Our intercourse being carried on
solely by means of the word, he who
falsifies that is a traitor to society"
("Of Giving the Lie"). "Lying is an
accursed vice," Montaigne declared.
And then he added, warming to his
subject with rather extraordinary
intensity, "If we did but recognize the
horror and gravity of . . . [lying], we
should punish it with flames more

justly than other crimes" ("Of Liars").
In other words, liars—more than
criminals of any other sort—deserve
to be burned at the stake.

Montaigne and Kant certainly had
a point. But they exaggerated. Effective social intercourse does not *strictly*
depend, as they maintained, on people telling one another the truth (not
as, say, respiration *strictly depends* on
oxygen, being *altogether impossible*
without it); nor does conversation
really lose *all* of its value when people
lie (some real information might
come through, and the entertainment
value of the conversation might even
be increased). After all, the amount
of lying and misrepresentation of all
kinds that actually goes on in the
world (of which the immeasurable
flood of bullshit is itself no more than

a fractional part) is enormous, and
yet productive social life manages
somehow to continue. The fact that
people often engage in lies, and in
other kinds of fraudulent behavior,
hardly renders it impossible to benefit
either from living with them or from
talking with them. It only means that
we have to be careful.

We can quite successfully find our
way through an environment of falsehood and fraud, as long as we can
reasonably count on our own ability
to discriminate reliably between
instances in which people are misrep-
resenting things to us and instances
in which they are dealing with us
straight. General confidence in the
truthfulness of others is not essential,
then, as long as we are justified in

having a certain sort of confidence in ourselves.

To be sure, we are rather easily fooled. Moreover, we know this to be the case. So it is not very easy for us to acquire and to sustain a secure and justifiable trust in our ability to spot attempts at deception. For this reason, social intercourse would indeed be severely burdened by a widespread and wanton disrespect for truth. However, our interest in shielding society from this burden is not what provides us with our most fundamental reason for caring about truth.

When we encounter people who lie to us, or who in some other way manifest a disregard for truth, it tends to anger and upset us. But it does not primarily do so, as Mon-

taigne and Kant would presumably
have had it, because we fear that the
mendacity we have encountered
threatens or encumbers the order of
society. Our main concern is clearly
not the concern of a *citizen*. What is
most immediately aroused in our
response to the liar is not *public spirit*.
It's something more personal. As a
rule, except perhaps when people
misrepresent matters in which serious public interests are directly
involved, we are dismayed far less by
the harm liars may be doing to the
general welfare than by their conduct
toward ourselves. What stirs us
against them, whether or not they
have somehow managed to betray all
of humankind, is that they have certainly injured us.

VII

How *do* lies injure us? Actually, as everyone knows, there are many familiar circumstances in which lies are not truly injurious to us at all. They may sometimes even be, on the whole, genuinely beneficial. For instance, a lie may protect us in one way or another from becoming aware of certain states of affairs, when no one (including ourselves) has anything in particular to gain from our being aware of them and when our awareness of them would cause us or others serious distress. Or, a lie may divert us from embarking upon a course of action that we find tempting but that would in fact lead to our doing ourselves more harm than good. Clearly, we must sometimes acknowledge that, all things considered, having been told a lie was actually helpful to us.

Even so, we often feel at such times that there was surely *something* bad about what the liar did. In the circumstances, it may be reasonable for us to be grateful for the lie. Whatever good the lie may turn out to have done, however, we believe at bottom that it would have been still better if its beneficial effects could have been achieved by sticking to the truth, without any recourse to lying.

The most irreducibly bad thing about lies is that they contrive to interfere with, and to impair, our natural effort to apprehend the real state of affairs. They are designed to prevent us from being in touch with what is really going on. In telling his lie, the liar tries to mislead us into believing that the facts are other than they actually are. He tries to impose his will on us. He aims at inducing us to accept his fabrication as an accurate account of how the world truly is.

Insofar as he succeeds in this, we acquire a view of the world that has its source in his imagination rather than being directly and reliably grounded in the relevant facts. The world we live in, insofar as our understanding of it is fashioned by the lie, is an imaginary world. There may be worse places to live; but this imaginary world won't do for us, at all, as a permanent residence.

Lies are designed to damage our grasp of reality. So they are intended, in a very real way, to make us crazy. To the extent that we believe them, our minds are occupied and governed by fictions, fantasies, and illusions that have been concocted for us by the liar. What we accept as real is a world that others cannot see, touch, or experience in any direct way. A person who believes a lie is constrained by it, accordingly, to live "in his own world"—a world that others cannot enter, and in which even the liar himself does not truly reside. Thus, the victim of the lie is, in the degree of his deprivation of truth, shut off from the world of common experience and isolated in an illusory realm to which there is no path that others might find or follow.

Truth and caring about truth concern us, then, in ways that do not bear simply upon our quotidian practical interests. They have a deeper and more damaging significance as well. One of the most rewarding of contemporary poets, Adrienne Rich, offers an account of the malign effect that lying inevitably has—apart from its harmful effect on the person to whom the lie is told—on the liar himself. With poetic exactitude, she observes that "the liar leads an existence of unutterable loneliness" ("Women and Honor: Some Notes on Lying," in Adrienne Rich, *Lies, Secrets, and Silence* [New York, 1979], p. 191). The loneliness is precisely *unutterable* because the liar cannot even reveal that he *is* lonely—that there is no one in his fabricated world—without disclosing, in doing so, that he has lied. He hides his own thoughts, pretending to believe what he does not believe, and thereby he makes it impossible for other people to be fully in touch with him. They cannot respond to him as he really is. They cannot even be aware that they are not doing so.

The liar refuses to permit himself, to the extent that he lies, to be known. This is an insult to his victims. It naturally injures their pride. For it denies them access to an elementary mode of human intimacy that is normally taken more or less for granted: the intimacy that consists in knowing what is on, or what is in, another person's mind.

In certain cases, Rich notes, lies may cause an even more profound sort of damage. "To discover that one has been lied to in a personal relationship," she says, "leads one to feel a little crazy" (*Lies, Secrets, and Silence,* p. 186). Here again, her observation is perspicuous. When we are dealing with someone whom we hardly know, we have to make a more or less deliberate assessment of his reliability in order to satisfy ourselves that what he tells us coincides with what he actually believes; and this assessment ordinarily pertains only to certain specific assertions that he has made. With our close friends, on the other hand, both of these conditions are usually relaxed. We suppose that our friends are generally honest with us, and we take this pretty much for granted. We tend to trust whatever they say, and we do so, mainly, not on the basis of a calculation establishing that they are currently telling us the truth, but because we feel comfortable and safe with them. As we familiarly put it, "We *just know* that they wouldn't lie to us."

With friends, the expectation of access and intimacy has become natural. It is grounded not in a calculated judgment but in our feelings—that is, in our subjective experience, rather than in any intellectual assessment based on pertinent objective data. It would be too much to say that our inclination to trust our friends belongs to our essential nature. But it could properly enough be said, as we sometimes do in fact say, that trusting

them has come to be "second nature"
to us.

That is why, as Rich observes,
discovering that a friend has lied to us
engenders in us a feeling of being a
little crazy. The discovery exposes
to us something about *ourselves*—
something far more disturbing than
merely that we have miscalculated, or
that we have made an error of judgment. It reveals that *our own nature*
(i.e., our *second* nature) is unreliable,
having led us to count on someone
whom we should not have trusted. It
shows us that we cannot realistically
be confident of our own ability to
distinguish truth from falsity—our
ability, in other words, to recognize
the difference between what is real
and what is not. Successfully deceiv-

ing a friend implies, needless to say, a
fault in the one who tells the lie.
However, it also shows that the victim
of the deception is defective too. The
liar betrays him, but he is betrayed by
his own feelings as well.

Self-betrayal pertains to craziness
because it is a hallmark of the irrational. The heart of rationality is to be
consistent; and being consistent, in
action or in thought, entails at least
proceeding so as not to defeat oneself. Aristotle suggested that an agent
acts rationally insofar as he conforms
his actions to the "mean"—that is, to
a point midway between excess and
deficiency. Suppose that, for the sake
of good health, someone follows a
diet that is either so meager or so
indulgent that it not only *fails to
improve* his health but actually leads

him to become *less healthy* than he
was. Aristotle urged that it is in this
defeat of his own purpose, in this self-
betrayal, that the *practical irrationality*
of the person's divergence from the
mean consists.

Intellectual activity is undermined,
similarly, by *logical* incoherence. When
a line of thought generates a contradic-
tion, its further progressive elabora-
tion is blocked. In whatever direction
the mind turns, it is driven back: it
must affirm what it has already re-
jected, or it must deny what it has
already affirmed. Thus, like behavior
that frustrates its own ambition,
contradictory thinking is irrational
because it defeats itself.

When a person discovers that he
has been told a lie by someone in
whose reliability he had found it

natural to have confidence, this shows him that he cannot rely on his own settled feelings of trust. He sees that he has been betrayed, in his effort to identify people in whom he can have confidence, by his own natural inclinations. These have led him to miss the truth rather than to attain it.

His assumption that he could guide himself in accordance with his own nature has turned out to be self-defeating, and hence irrational. Since he finds that he is by nature out of touch with reality, he may well feel that he is a little crazy.

VIII

However penetrating and illuminating Rich's thoughts about lying in personal relationships may appear to be, there is in this matter, as of course there is in almost every matter, more than one side to the coin. Another wonderful poet—perhaps, in fact, the greatest of all—has a rather different tale to tell. Here is Shakespeare's charming and provocative sonnet 138:

When my love swears that she is made of truth,
I do believe her though I know she lies,

That she might think me some untutored youth,
Unlearn'd in the world's false subtleties.
Thus vainly thinking that she thinks me young,
Although she knows my days are past the best,
Simply I credit her false-speaking tongue:
On both sides thus is simple truth suppressed.
But wherefore says she not she is unjust?
And wherefore say not I that I am old?
O, love's best habit is in seeming trust,
And age in love loves not to have years told.
Therefore I lie with her and she with me,
And in our faults by lies we flattered be.

There is a widely accepted dogma according to which it is essential for lovers to trust each other. Shakespeare is doubtful. His observation in the sonnet is that the best thing for lovers—"love's best habit"—is actually not *genuine* trust. Mere "*seeming* trust" is just as good, he suggests, if not sometimes even better.

The woman in Shakespeare's poem professes to be utterly truthful—she "swears that she is made of truth"—yet she lyingly pretends to believe that the man is younger than she knows him to be. The man knows that she doesn't really believe this, but he decides to accept her characterization of herself as truthful. So he brings himself to think that she really does believe the lie about his age that he has told her, and thus that she really does consider him to be younger than he actually is.

She lies to him about how honest she is, and about believing his account of his age. He lies to her about how old he is, and about whether he

accepts her representation of herself
as thoroughly truthful. Each of them
knows all of this: each knows that the
other is lying, and both know that
their own lies are not believed. Each
lyingly pretends to believe, however,
that the other is flawlessly straight-
forward. This collection of lies
enables the two lovers, united in
"seeming trust," to believe that their
self-flattering lies about themselves—
as impeccably honest, or as engag-
ingly youthful—have been accepted.
And thus, lying with each other in
this way, they conclude in lying happily together.

I suggested earlier that part of the
fault in lying is that the liar, by denying access to what is truly in or on his
mind, forecloses an elementary and
normally presumed mode of human

intimacy. That foreclosure is surely
not a feature of the situation Shakespeare describes. The lovers in his
sonnet know not only what is in each
other's mind but what lies behind it as
well. Each knows what the other is
really thinking. And each knows that
the other knows this: they lie egre-
giously to each other, but neither is
fooled. Each knows that the other is
lying, and each is aware that his or her
own lies are seen through.

Neither of the lovers is actually
getting away with anything. Both
comprehend what is really going on
in the mirrored and layered complex
of attempted deceptions that they
have severally contrived. Everything
is reassuringly transparent to them.
Both of the lovers are secure in their
awareness that their love is undam-

aged by their lies. They can see, through all the lies they have been told, and through all the lies they themselves have told, that their love survives even knowing the truth.

My guess is that the intimacy these lying lovers share, in virtue of recognizing each other's lies and in virtue also of knowing that their own lies have not successfully deceived, is especially deep and enjoyable. The intimacy they achieve spreads to corners of themselves that they have made specific and potentially costly efforts to keep hidden. Despite it all, however, they see that they have seen through each other. The hidden corners of each have been penetrated. The realization by each of them that each both occupies and is occupied by the other, and that this mutual pene-

tration of their lies has marvelously
led their exercises of deception to the
truth of love, must be wonderfully
delicious.

I do not ordinarily recommend or
condone lying. In most cases, I am
all for truth. Nevertheless, if you are
confident that you can lie yourself into
a situation like the one Shakespeare
sketches in his sonnet, my advice to
you is: Go for it!

IX

Truth possesses instrumental value when it is taken, as it were, in separate pieces. After all, it is specific, individual truths that are useful. The pragmatic value of truth is manifested for the engineer in statements concerning such things as the tensile strength and elasticity of materials, for the physician in statements concerning, let us say, white blood cell counts, for the astronomer in descriptions of the trajectories of heavenly bodies, and so on.

None of these seekers and

employers of truth is necessarily concerned with truth *as such*. They care primarily about the discrete facts, and about inferences that these facts may support. This does not require them to care about the abstract notions of *factuality* or of *truth*. They are curious about truths concerning facts that belong to a specific domain of inquiry. Their curiosity is satisfied when they have acquired a set of what they consider to be true, and therefore useful, beliefs about the particular topics in which they are especially interested.

But what can be said about the value of *truth itself,* as distinct from the rather commonplace suggestions I have already offered concerning the value of individual truths? As a start, let's get clear about what we are asking when we ask about the value of truth itself, or when we ask what reason there is for us to care about truth *as such.* Even before that, indeed, we really should get clear about *what it means*—concretely and as a practical matter—to value and to care about *truth* in the first place. What does caring about truth, as distinct from caring merely about the acquisition and exploitation of specific truths, actually come to?

For one thing, of course, a person who cares about truth cares about the strengthening and extension of our grasp of particular truths, especially of truths that are particularly interesting or that are likely to be particularly valuable. Caring about truth entails other things as well: finding satisfaction, and perhaps the special joy of the lover, in recognizing and in understanding significant truths that were previously unknown or obscure; being eager to protect, from distortion and discredit, our appreciation of those truths that we already possess; and, in general, being determined to encourage within society, insofar as we are able to do so, a vigorous and stable preference for true beliefs over ignorance, error, doubt, and misrepresentation. There is every reason to suppose that these ambitions are heartily shared by those who devote themselves to searching for specific truths about particular subjects. Indeed, it would be difficult to find anyone at all to whom these ambitions would seem unworthy.

In any event, caring about truth plays a considerably different role in our lives, and in our culture, than does caring about the accumulation of individual truths. It has a deeper and a more general significance. It provides a ground and a motivation for our curiosity about the facts and for our commitment to the importance of inquiry. It is because we appreciate that truth is important to us that we care about accumulating truths.

This does little more, I must admit, than to reiterate my old story about the utility of truth. However, there is an additional story to tell here. It is a more richly philosophical story that does not pertain just to our practical needs and interests.

We learn that we are separate beings in the world, distinct from what is other than ourselves, by coming up against obstacles to the fulfill-

ment of our intentions——that is, by
running into opposition to the implementation of our will. When certain
aspects of our experience fail to
submit to our wishes, when they are
on the contrary unyielding and even
hostile to our interests, it then
becomes clear to us that they are not
parts of ourselves. We recognize that
they are not under our direct and
immediate control; instead, it
becomes apparent that they are inde-
pendent of us. That is the origin of
our concept of reality, which is essentially a concept of what limits us, of
what we cannot alter or control by
the mere movement of our will.

To the extent that we learn in
greater detail how we are limited,
and what the limits of our limitation
are, we come thereby to delineate our

own boundaries and thus to discern
our own shape. We learn what we can
and cannot do, and the sorts of effort
we must make in order to accomplish
what is actually possible for us. We
learn our powers and our vulnerabili-
ties. This not only provides us with an
even more emphatic sense of our
separateness. It defines for us the
specific sort of being that we are.

Thus, our recognition and understanding of our own identity arises
out of, and depends integrally on, our
appreciation of a reality that is defini-
tively independent of ourselves. In
other words, it arises out of and
depends on our recognition that there
are facts and truths over which we
cannot hope to exercise direct or
immediate control. If there were no
such facts or truths, if the world

invariably and unresistingly became
whatever we might like or wish it
to be, we would be unable to distinguish ourselves from what is other
than ourselves and we would have
no sense of what in particular we
ourselves are. It is only through our
recognition of a world of stubbornly
independent reality, fact, and truth
that we come both to recognize ourselves as beings distinct from others
and to articulate the specific nature
of our own identities.

How, then, can we fail to take the
importance of factuality and of reality
seriously? How can we fail to care
about truth?

We cannot.